SECRETS OF LIFE BEFORE FORM

A look beyond the façade of human existence

TAPIWA CHITEMBURE

Secrets of Life Before Form

A look beyond the façade of human existence

ISBN: 979-8-9878878-0-6

Published by Digital Mint, LLC

Publishing date: 5/8/2023

Book cover image credits: Adobe Express.

Book cover concept and design by Tapiwa Chitembure

TABLE OF CONTENTS

SPIRIT

FORM   PURPOSE

DEDICATION

I dedicate this book to you, the reader. May you find the truth you seek and the freedom that it brings!

INTRODUCTION

After writing the book Subtle Affirmations, I realized there was part of the story of life that kept illuding my awareness. Since I generally like to finish what I start, I could not leave this mystery hanging. For me, spirituality is a search to find and experience life's steadfast truths. Knowing that any real truth must be indispensable to existence allowed me to realize that spiritual truths must be with us in every moment. Therefore, as human beings, we must have adopted and continue to perpetuate misconceptions of life that blind us from the truth. One of those misconceptions is the idea that life begins at conception.

Except for those who already have life figured out, there is a lot that remains for us to discover about existence on our philosophical or spiritual journeys. Personally, I find that as I continue to grow spiritually, more questions and revelations flood my awareness. Occasionally, I hit a real mind bender of a mystery that when resolved, reveals a long-forgotten perspective of life, which in turn restores a long-neglected truth of life. What I want to share with you can certainly feel like a mind bender. But I assure you that what makes it a mind bender is not the truth, but spiritual misconceptions courtesy of our human existence, false knowledge, and beliefs.

What you are about to explore is nothing new, but it's one of the most elusive and therefore most omitted or overlooked parts of the story of life. Our understanding of life and our grasp of what makes life after death an actuality is limited without taking into consideration the nature of life before birth. And no, I don't mean prenatal experiences when I say life before birth. I mean before life (the source of *conscious activity*), takes up form. So, we are looking into life in its purest state before the inception of any life organisms or any reproductive conception.

As humanity, we often fixate and think about the subject of life after death more than we think about the *essence* of life before the genesis of form. We believe that life begins at reproductive conception. But could it be possible that only the reproduction of form begins at conception, but a fully functioning entity already exists before that?

To put things in perspective, we can all agree that there will be no point in inventing a car if the car did not have a function value, right? So, the *purpose* of a car would precede the invention or creation of a car, agreed? Who a specific car will serve may remain unknown. But what drives the invention of the car is the awareness that the car will be of service to *someone*, correct? Therefore, because a car needs a driver, we can rightfully conclude that Henry Ford wouldn't have created a car if there was no one for the car to serve.

Similarly, we can theorize that life forms exist to serve the needs of something that is formless. This opens the possibility that we may be wrong in defining life in terms of the conception or the evolution of form alone. As a result, we must look beyond the façade of human form to discover the essence of life, i.e., the nature of the "consumer" who benefits from the function value or purpose that is unique to form.

What if someone said the car and the driver are one, and they all come from the same assembly line, would you find that agreeable? My guess is that you may find such a proposition too illogical to process. So, if we were to consider the process from conception to birth as a natural assembly line, would it be rational to think the spirit is "made" on that assembly line?

If we believe that the spirit is made through conception, we might as well believe that the spirit is created by evolution, because evolution is the destiny of such a belief. Spirituality cannot be logical under the premise of evolution. However, evolution can still be logical as part of the process of creation under the premise that life came into being from the activities of a *formless* conscious entity or entities.

4

Because we *habitually* believe that the life of an individual begins at conception, there is so much that remains unknown to us about the essence of life. Unless we realize that conception or birth do not mark the beginning of the story of life, we will remain in the dark about the needs or function value that inspired the creation of form. Moreover, we will hide from our awareness the intrinsic nature of those whom the creation of form benefits. The way I see it, such an omission eventually leads to spiritual oblivion, as you too may discover.

Oblivion is one of the points on the Spectrum of Conclusions Chart, which I first introduced in the book Subtle Affirmations. Just to give you a brief rundown, this chart evolved from my realization that every conclusion we make has the potential to increase or decrease our scope of awareness. The idea behind the Spectrum of Conclusions Chart is that a conclusion is only as true as it mirrors the essence of something. And the more a conclusion departs from the truth the more it impedes our awareness, and therefore is a lie, in other words, an awareness obstacle.

Before we move on, I must point out that not all lies are intentional or formed with malintent. Even an innocent misunderstanding can be a lie. How come? Because a lie distorts the meaning, idea, or awareness of the essence of something. So, when I talk about a lie, I am mostly referring to anything that can hide, distort, or prevent our awareness of the truth, case in point, the idea that "life begins at conception." That conception is a relative beginning of form is a fact. However, I think conception is much further in the chain of events to allow us any insights into the *reasons* that necessitated the creation of life forms.

One of the realizations that still blows my mind about the Spectrum of Conclusions Chart, is how it reveals the fact that any conclusion we make within the premise of falsehoods will diminish our awareness. While any conclusions we arrive at from a premise that mirrors or approximates the essence of life does the opposite, which is increase our understanding or awareness of life. Because the Spectrum of Conclusions Chart helps us to be *impartial* and objective, it is a valuable tool that I am sure any genuine truth seeker will appreciate. So, it is only fitting that I share this chart with you once again as we embark on a journey that will most likely put your convictions to the test. I will dive into the Spectrum of Conclusions Chart a bit later to give you a better orientation on its use.

In the search for truth, it is not uncommon to start with speculation, belief, or even facts. But if we are going to establish the truth, we cannot start and end with speculations, beliefs, or facts. Because even facts can be misleading, especially when it comes to spiritual matters. For example, the fact that there are many human races does not necessarily mean that race is an aspect of our spiritual nature. We can learn all about race and still be oblivious of our spiritual nature. We will be no closer to discovering the essence of life if we only focus or rationalize life based on race. So, this fact alone tells us that we must seek insights that transcend race or in this case—form.

In a world full of uncertainties, facts become a comfort zone for most people. However, we must realize that sometimes lies persist with the blessings of facts. In other words, the very same facts that we find comfort in can impede our awareness of life's core qualities. Spiritual truths belong to those who dare to question the nature of existence beyond what is visible. The truth is earned by those willing to pursue it outside of the blinding loop of stagnant beliefs. Only those who are not fixed in materialistic logic can embrace it. And only those who seek to understand life first and foremost, rather than be right, can be nourished by the truth.

Yes, it can be nerve wracking to explore life untethered from popular beliefs. However, if we worship popular ideas, facts, or beliefs simply out of fear of being alone or being ostracized by society for pursuing truth, we can blind ourselves by our approval of conclusions that impede our spiritual growth. Materialistic facts omit the WHYs and HOWs of life. They are too fixed or rigid to explain parts of life that are not physical, like thought, emotion, dreams, or any other type of conscious activity. For those reasons, we cannot depend on materialistic philosophies to gain a comprehensive understanding of life.

After having an out-of-body experience when I was 10, I struggled to make sense of it first because I had very limited knowledge on the matter. Secondly, I could not talk about what happened to me, not even indirectly, without someone coming to some premature conclusions on the matter. But, in the moment that I saw my body as an entity that is distinct from me, I experienced bliss and freedom beyond words. It is then when I first realized that I was formless, and that form alone does not equate to existence. Consequently, I also realized that consciousness without form does not equate to non-existence. As similar events happened throughout my life, I knew I had to find out what was going on with me.

So, I started searching for answers, and that spiritual journey is what inspired the book Subtle Affirmations.

While I feel lucky to have found the affirmation of my spiritual nature through my out-of-body experiences, what I've gained the most from these experiences is a perspective that allowed me to see and understand life looking in from the outside. So, I want to ask you to assume that perspective as you read this book. Only then will any insights, revelations, or thoughts that I share with you make sense.

Revelations are the truth coming forward in a natural manner. An example of a revelation is an affirmable realization that naturally comes to you as you consider a question. The way to know if an answer is true is whether the answer satisfies the question in a way that *you* can affirm. Revelations come from the power of knowing that lies within each one of us. This power predates formal education in human history.

Why should we care that the power of revelations predates formal education? Here are my thoughts on that. Reason is the most fundamental way in which we interact with life and get some insights about it. As a truth seeker, you must realize that knowledge evolves from questions, reason, observation, experiences, and affirmation. Formal education does not always aid us in this process. The ancient Greeks did not figure out that Earth was round from formal education. Explorers and mathematicians may have affirmed that the Earth was indeed round. But what made it possible to examine and validate the conclusion that the Earth was round, is a power that is native to all of us, the power to consider or observe life with the purpose of understanding it. Unless you return to this foundation of knowledge, it can be easy for you to doubt your observations when you come up against popular beliefs. So, the search for truth requires that you always guard yourself against anything that can impair your awareness.

True, it will be a difficult task for anyone to try and figure out life from scratch. So, education has its value! But because formal education is not always amenable to free thought or revelations, that can make it seem like your own insights into life don't matter. This is where formal education ruins our ability to gain insights from life naturally.

The fact that some of the most brilliant minds in history are dropouts should tell you something. If you look at our educational system, it's ironic that you can find curriculums built on discoveries made by dropouts, or some technology invented by a dropout, like Thomas Edison. To reiterate, I am not saying education isn't important, not at all! Nevertheless, if we ignore the fact that a rigid system of education has its limits in our pursuit of life's insights, we will suffer in silence learning things that we are not passionate about. What this teaches us is that there are many paths to knowledge. Ultimately, knowledge begins with curiosity before any path of learning is relevant.

I wish I'd known sooner that the focus of our educational systems is to develop career paths, not to answer life's deepest mysteries. I would have at least retained my freedom of thought without feeling like I was the odd man out. When institutions of learning or religion assume the role of the all-knowing authority, you may feel inferior or out of place when you cannot find support for your revelations, or a way to process things that you are curious about without insults to your state of mind. So, the sooner you realize that you may not find support for your revelations within institutions of learning or rigid religious systems, the better you will be. Otherwise, they will nullify your curiosity or revelations before you can even process them to determine the truth.

At this time, our formal education is designed in such a way that you cannot bear witness to your own experiences or revelations. This is trained into you through the process of having you provide citations to support your ideas. And through that process, your natural discoveries or revelations can become mute as a valid source of insight. So, unless you stay clear minded and you stay true to yourself, you may find yourself feeling uninspired. There might be a sense of community in singing the same tune in the choir of popular ideology. But that is the very mindset that has kept us blind of our timeless qualities.

Popular ideology can only have the power to hijack your awareness when you think little of your revelations. Even when you doubt your own insights, it's better that you evaluate the premise of your doubts than to simply give in to what is popular. Such a one-sided compromise might work to keep the peace, but it becomes costly when it prevents you from discovering your very own essence. Since the subject of this book might be unpalatable for some, I thought I should warn you that you may feel like the odd one out. That is normal for spiritual awakenings. So, don't give up easily if you can't find wide consensus. But I am hopeful, because despite all the doom and gloom in the media, the world is going through an awakening. The status-quo of spiritless ideology is failing to account for human behaviors that suggest spiritual distress. As a result, people have a thirst for deeper insights into life. So, the world will have to return to its spiritual roots, because spirituality is truly as deep as life goes.

In the spectrum of all there is to know, spirituality is like a staircase of life's truths from the chaos of our human existence, towards our spiritual autonomy and truest individuality. In spite of the modern tools that we can use to examine life, we really gain knowledge through reason, observation, by asking questions, or through accidental discoveries. I think the most meaningful knowledge for us as individuals, is knowledge that empowers us *truthfully*, born out of genuine questions. When a question is well placed, and it ignites a thirst or hunger for deep insights, revelations or breakthroughs can be possible. The moral of the story is do not underestimate the power of your questions. A question can be your call to an awakening or revelation.

While reading this book you may experience an identity metamorphosis. That is normal since all that is not you tends to fall away as you awaken to your true nature. So, do not be alarmed. Just keep pushing through. Freedom is the summit of truth. But the resolve to reach that summit is in your hands! You may find that there is a lot you might have to unlearn to get to the truth. Realize that too is part of your spiritual revival. Since there are many layers to spiritual awareness, I recommend that you read this book as many times as you need to satisfy any questions you might have. Without further ado, let's dive right in!

THE SPECTRUM OF CONCLUSIONS

A conclusion is a final judgement of some kind. It can be an idea or an opinion that we come to with the information that is available to us. And it can also be a concept, decision, or mindset that symbolizes a plateau of awareness on a given subject. Given that in life we will encounter both truths and lies, we need to give ourselves the freedom to adjust our conclusions as we learn more about things. Without this freedom, we can weaken our awareness.

Ideally, in our attempts to understand life, we want to reach a point of awareness that is in harmony with the essence of existence, and that we know as the truth. The flipside of that would be conclusions that impede our awareness of the essence of life, and those we know as lies.

As people who consume information, we need to understand that the conclusions that we make establish the direction, freedom, or limitations of our awareness. The essence of the truth is that it reveals the nature of the subject, or dispels a mystery, thereby elevating our awareness. And the essence of lies is that they hide the nature of the subject, thereby oppressing our awareness and creating a mystery. Ironically, even to know a lie, we must understand the nature of a lie.

For anything to be unknown, something must hide it from our grasp. On the other hand, we may assume that something exists, when nothing of the sort exists. Thus, it remains "unknown." The latter is common in false or superstitious beliefs. So, the Spectrum of Conclusions Chart comes in handy as a tool that can help us sort through this mess by evaluating how comprehensively our ideas, opinions, beliefs, etc., mirror life or not. *See complete chart on page 120.*

The *rationale* of the Spectrum of Conclusions Chart is that the more you approach the truth, the more your conclusions will align with the nature of what you are trying to understand. And the more you encounter lies, the more that you will become unaware of the essence of what you are trying to understand. I am still trying to figure out the natural order for the states of mind at the bottom of the chart. But I hope as is, the chart gives you some idea of the *relationship* between our awareness and the conclusions that we make. I also included a simpler version of the chart that you will find at the end of this chapter. So, you can play around with these charts until you get a good sense of how the spectrum works.

Truth and lies can alter our state of awareness, and so too can our own conclusions, depending on where they fall on the side of truth or lies. I have affirmed through my experiences that the truth has the power to set us free indeed. But that is not all the truth does. The truth also has the power to unite us by our fundamental nature. Without the truth, life becomes a lonely and sometimes contentious journey in which we isolate ourselves in our own unique experiences, unable to find the link of truth that connects us to each other.

Whenever you find yourself in a lopsided relationship with someone, it's likely because of the differences in your states of awareness. I am willing to bet that every parent raising a child gets this lopsided feeling to some degree. That's because they are dealing not only with little people, but also individuals who are unaware of how to survive by themselves. This is not to say kids are not spiritually aware. But they can easily get confused by all the visuasions[1] of this world. Anyway, the parent must facilitate the means to nurture that child's awareness, in addition to providing other forms of sustenance. This means the parents themselves must possess a level of awareness that will allow them to help each child navigate the challenges of life in form and in spirit. Therefore, I think what each parent hopes

---

[1] **Visuasions** is a word coined by Tapiwa Chitembure. It is short for *visual persuasions*. Used by Tapiwa to express the tendency in form-based reality to overshadow spiritual or formless aspects of life.

to do is find points where their awareness coincides with their child's awareness, and then gradually build a bond in their awareness of life's truths with each child. I can tell you, sometimes, that is easier said than done, especially when the truth is not known by one or both parties in any relationship.

The truth implies uniformity of essence in every instance of existence within a similar set of conditions. This means that we cannot use our personal experiences as a standard for truth. For example, I had an out-of-body experience that made me realize my spiritual nature. Someone else might have a near death experience that makes them distinguish their spiritual essence from their body. And another person may recall a past life which affirms a distinction between the body and the spirit. I may have no recall of a past life or a near death experience. However, when I look closely at each of these experiences, I can find a common thread that suggest the nature of the spirit; and that is a state or potential for awareness that is independent of form. That is the truth that connects this wide array of spiritual experiences.

When you are looking for spiritual truths, it's the common thread that matters. Your unique experiences that lead you to a certain truth are symbolic of your path to the truth, not the truth itself. Therefore, in the same vein, when we argue about religion instead of finding the common thread in every religion, we will undoubtably end up obscuring spiritual truths that can revive us from the core, despite of the religious label that truth may fall under. So, in using the Spectrum of Conclusions Chart, we are essentially trying to filter out the noise caused by each of our unique experiences, opinions, or beliefs, so that we can identify a common thread, in other words, the truth! I hope that you will keep that in mind as you move through this book. I do not wish for my experiences to come across as better than anyone else's experience. Because they are simply points of reference that explain how I got to the conclusions of the truths that I am certain are part of your essence as well!

Life has taught me that it takes humility to break through the blind spots that keep us from discovering life's core truths. The Spectrum of Conclusions Chart can be an eye-opening tool in this regard. When used in good faith, this chart can help you undo the convictions that do not align with your core qualities. Consequently, as you elevate your awareness towards the top of the chart, you might find yourself inseparable from the core truth that lies have been obscuring. Without consciousness, *the* truth cannot exist! Therefore, lies seek to *undermine* consciousness in order to have staying power. Unless you look at the basis of your conclusions, you may lend your power to ideas or beliefs that work against your core individuality. By now, I am sure you can figure out where that leads to with the Spectrum of Conclusions Chart.

SPECTRUM OF CONCLUSIONS CHART SIMPLIFIED

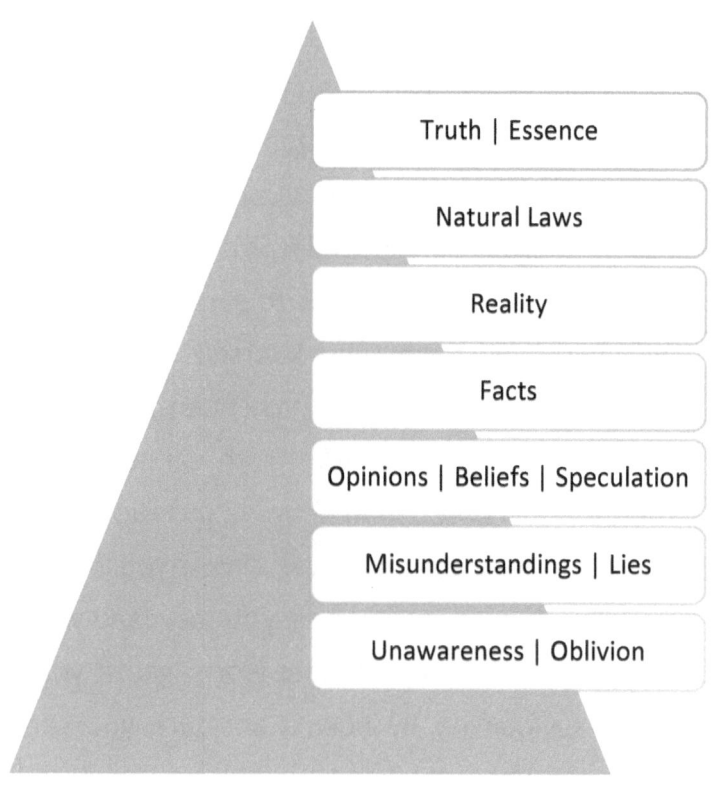

Truth | Essence

Natural Laws

Reality

Facts

Opinions | Beliefs | Speculation

Misunderstandings | Lies

Unawareness | Oblivion

WHAT DEFINES YOU?

B efore we can wrap our heads around the possibility of life before birth, we must first address the elephant in the room, and that is the fact of our human existence. From what I could deduce from my out of body experiences, it is my understanding that what we know as life exists within an intricate balance between the material and spiritual realms. Just like some plant life exists within a delicate balance of earth, water and sunlight, human existence is an intricate balance between body, mind, and spirit.

Some plants struggle to grow where there is too much or too little sunshine, too much or too little water, or where the earth is too hard or too soft to support the plant's roots. From this we can deduce that the unique elements that form life must come together in an intricate balance to support life. So, life as we see it in plants or in animal life, is a byproduct of different elements coming together. Some elements may hold a distinct form, and some may hold no form at all. But that does not mean they don't exist.

The same is true for us as individuals. There are different elements that make up our animated human form. Each of those elements serve a unique function that balances what is lacking in the other. If we can examine or meditate on the differences between each of these elements, we will start to understand and appreciate the nature of each element that leads to the manifestation of human existence.

If you look at a human being within the model of things that have form versus things that do not have form, it's obvious that you will place the human body along with things that hold form. But would you place consciousness, intelligence, or our potential for thought along with things that hold form?

I am going to diverge for a little bit to share with you a story that will help me unpack my insights on the theme of identity. A friend of mine recently asked me how I cope with racism, meaning me being a black man. Now, this may come as a surprise to some people, but the fact that I am a black man is not at the forefront of how I see myself. In fact, I hardly think about it until someone points this out to me. This is not to say racism doesn't exist. I just mean that I give the fact of my race as much value as a race car driver would attribute the performance of his or her car on the paint job. In other words, my race is not a huge factor in the scope of the things that give me my sense of existence or the extent of my potential. And I think I am not the only one who feels this way.

Instances of racism may flare up in our society. But I believe the rest of the rational world is ready to move away from racism, since racism is too painful for any rational mind to dwell on. While we must not turn a blind eye on racism, we must

27

be careful not to generalize racism in a way that is unfair to our spiritual allies, those who see beyond skin color. Not everyone that doesn't like crime joins the police force. So, we can also expect that not everyone that finds racism despicable is going to turn into an activist. We all process pain differently. Therefore, we must not assume that someone's silence means they are complicit in racism. It's better to suggest how others can help than to cause further division with unfounded accusations.

Anyway, from a spiritual perspective, while my spiritual awareness is not a coping mechanism for racism, it just happens to be the very thing that has pulled me out of thinking that the color of my skin bears any value to my fundamental nature. I cannot help it if someone believes that the color of my skin should decide my place in society. But that does not mean that I must give such misguided notions any validity.

Being aware of what I am beyond what people can see has given me some insights into the origins of racism. At the core of racism, or any form of injustice, you will find spiritual ignorance. Racism is a spiritual injustice perpetuated by those who have no idea what a spirit is and those who deny that such an entity even exists! It takes the conviction that we are nothing more than our bodies before racism can exist. And that is why I concluded that spiritual blindness must be a precondition that justifies racism and other forms of injustice.

If I defined or saw myself only as a black man in this world, I would give every racial sentiment the power to shape me or cut me down. So, I am grateful that through my spiritual awakening, I can take a step back and see racism for what it is. And so, I think the most efficient way to address racism is to address spiritual ignorance. I have no doubt that the rest will sort itself out.

I apologize if the topic of racism leaves anyone feeling uncomfortable. But my hope is that this story helps you realize how the things we believe define our identity can impact our mental health or attitude towards life. In other words, the parameters that we use to create our sense of identity can affect the scope of our awareness, which in turn affects our state of mind.

So, what is it that defines you in the truest sense? As human beings, we generally use two parameters to cultivate our sense of identity. These are genetic factors and environmental factors. Briefly, genetic factors represent all the makings of our physical potential and natural definitive characteristics, such as race and gender. The environment represents the setting or factors that tend to shape our mindset and potential into distinct traits or abilities. In this simplistic view, we sometimes bundle-in our potential for thought as genetically hereditary. Thus, any sense of identity that we derive from our genetic or environmental parameters will be along the lines of heritage, nationality, and the history and social status of our ancestors. It makes sense therefore that when we are trying to express our identity, we must look back at our family's history, right? We look at our culture, nationality, education, etc., and from that we say, "I am…" African, European, Middle Eastern, Asian, or whatever the case might be. In other words, we decide on our identity.

In the intellectual or creative arena, we may define ourselves by our career paths, or intellectual and creative passions. But in most cases, we keep our default identity within the parameters of the genetic and environmental factors which form the roots of our primary sense of identity. You don't have to take my word for it on this. If you are willing to talk to and listen to people, you will find that their heritage can be a big source of pride. But it can also be a source of disgrace, especially when we become attached to a heritage that has an undesirable past.

You may have looked at this identity structure at some point in your life and thought, "there's got to be more to life than this!" Well, if you did, you are not alone. When I was a young man, Billy Joel's song "the River of Dreams" became my spiritual journey's theme song. It struck a chord with me because I was at a point in my awakening where I was not sure what I was looking for. Later in life, I realized that I had been facing a void resulting from the fact that I could no longer satisfactorily define myself within genetic or environmental parameters. I felt that part of me was missing something when I only regarded myself within these two parameters.

Part of my mistake was thinking that I had to define myself in a way that would be acceptable to others, instead of embracing the revelations about my true nature. So, it turns out that I was subconsciously rejecting the very thing that I was looking for by doubting my revelations. I did not know peace within myself until I stopped evading my spiritual nature. And this brings me back to the point that I was getting to when I shared with you my thoughts on racism.

In a world that operates largely on materialistic parameters, those who operate on form driven logic only will be inclined to discriminate against anything formless or unseen as "not real" or "nonexistent." This is a type of rejection that nullifies the very core of life, the spirit. So, if the parameters that you use to define yourself do not approximate your core nature, you may find yourself deeply affected by any sentiment that does not acknowledge your spiritual nature. Life only has the power to nullify you, the same way racism might nullify any individual who only identifies themselves by race. In other words, the mental impact of any hardship that we face in life will only be great to the degree that we distance ourselves from our essence. On the other hand, if we can affirm and embrace our spiritual nature, we will also become resilient naturally as part of our eternal nature. So, from a very early stage, I started to consider myself as a conscious being with potential, because that made more sense to me than the idea that my brain had anything to do with who or what I am.

I will grant that the brain is the body's control center. But one of the most confounding parts of my first out-of-body experience, was me realizing that I was looking directly at my body. So, I quickly outgrew the misconception that my brain was the core of my awareness, and I have not been able to *fit into* the theory that the brain is the source of conscious activity ever since.

Spirituality goes against the grain of the earth-bound logic that seeks to reduce us down to flesh and bones. I could be wrong, but I believe that spirituality for most people begins with the suspicion that there must be an external entity with the potential to give life to form; before form becomes "alive." What we call that entity is not as important as our realization of what it does. So, once you know what it does, you may begin to get the suspicion that the entity that must exist before life can begin is...wait a minute, what's going on here? Yep! This may be a light-bulb moment for some! Embrace your awakening in this moment! Realize that you are that entity. Nothing between you and this page is capable of the conscious activity of understanding, but *you*!

At the core of your human existence, you, the spirit, are the conscious custodian tasked with the responsibility of monitoring and maintaining the intricate balance that makes life possible. This undoubtably is a task that you've had to perform with your hands tied, metaphorically speaking. And one of the things that helped to keep your hands tied was how you defined yourself. Since human relationships generally work on implicit agreements, it is not always easy to pull ourselves out of harmony with the ones we love. And this can become a trap for anyone that cannot navigate the challenges of being themselves while interacting with those who only define themselves by form.

Due to the variations in the parameters that every individual might use to define themselves, the concept of life before birth will not make sense to everyone. This does not nullify the prospect of life before birth being an actuality. Given that the parameters that we use to define ourselves can expand or limit the scope of our awareness, we must be willing to reevaluate the premise that life begins at conception. Because if we simply decide that life does not exist before conception based on our oblivion, we will leave ourselves with no recourse to the source of our vitality, the energy that gives life to form.

Being formless is not the same as nothingness. But our failure to acknowledge any characteristics that distinguish the formless part of life from life's form can create the illusion of "nothingness." We have materialistic logic to thank for that, since such logic only considers existence by juxtaposing the presence of form against the absence of form. Such an equation does not even account for the formless forces that drive life at all. However, those who adhere to this way of thinking will be quick to conclude that nothingness is an absolute. But how could that be true especially when their own equation omits or cannot account for things like consciousness or thought?

The concept of a spirit is one that has illuded mankind for thousands of years. A quick look at any religion known to humanity proves that we could not talk about spirits or Gods without humanizing them, in other words, giving them form. As a result, we have built a form-dependent way of thinking that is incapable of seeing how life might have originated from a formless creative entity or entities.

To illustrate what I mean, imagine yourself existing as pure consciousness, detached from your body. If you could do it at all, you may have found yourself feeling a bit uneasy about not being able to define yourself outside the context of form. That's what happened to me the more I thought about my out-of-body experience at first, without knowing *myself*. We define existence in terms of form to the extent that we despise being formless. To make matters worse, we have humanized spirituality to the extent that we may only imagine our spiritual selves as a transparent figure of our physical form. This can create perception challenges that can sidetrack anyone embarking on a spiritual journey from embracing their core state of existence.

In our search for truth, I think what we are essentially looking for is a combination of factors that give us a complete picture or understanding of life. Jesus offered us some clues about what the combination of factors that make up life are in the concept of the trinity. However, we have lost the true meaning behind the trinity because of our inclination to humanize spirituality. Thus, when Jesus spoke of the "Father," possibly to convey the existence of something with the potential for creating life, we humanized that with a literal idea of a man with a great white beard floating in the sky. So, what else could we have possibly misunderstood from what Jesus was trying to teach us?

The way I see it, the trinity is an equation that represents the essence of each of the three elements that go into forming a human being. Each of these three factors are essential to human existence. Therefore, they are equally important within the context of creating human lives, but they are not equal in rank or potential when it comes to the responsibility of living and giving life direction.

Early in this chapter I said life is an intricate balance between mind, body, and spirit; and that the spirit is responsible for maintaining that balance. How? By moderating its own intentions, the mind, and by moderating what the body does. We can say rationality is part of the process the spirit uses to keep life in balance. So, it's no wonder our world spirals into chaos when we nullify the spirit or treat it as an afterthought.

When we disregard the essence of an individual, we also diminish their ability to maintain life's balance. It's like blindfolding the driver while the car is going. That cannot end well! It makes you wonder what good any religion that tells you that you are nothing accomplishes. You cannot define yourself within the parameters of such a religion and honestly feel good about yourself. I tried it and it just felt wrong to the core!

Let's imagine God as a father in the literal sense for a moment. If he told you that you were nothing without him all the time, would you feel loved? If he made you feel unworthy of deciding on the purpose of your life, instead of showing you how to do it yourself, would you be much of an individual? If the answer is no, we can agree that someone misled us about God, or what his supposed intentions for us are. And that is why such a way of thinking cannot nourish the spirit enough to be free! So where do you think such beliefs fall on the Spectrum of Conclusions?

There are three ways that I know of in which an individual's freedom can be stolen. The first is physical enslavement. The second is using a position of authority unfairly to turn the society against an individual. And the third way, which I think is more insidious, is to distance you from your power and make you feel unworthy of giving your life purpose and direction.

As a father myself, I look forward to the day when my kids can safely fly out of the coup. That does not mean I don't love them. The love I have for my kids drives me to do all I can to prepare each of them as an individual to hopefully make good choices, so they can make it on their own. In other words, I want them to be free! If they choose to learn from my life's experiences and strive to do even better than I did, I will worry less. But, if they want freedom first, without knowing how to be free, I would be worried. Because I know life can be a cruel teacher! So, if I cannot be their mentor, life, or someone without their best interest at heart will step in. However, even as a father, I would not raise my kids as an absolute authority.

Sure, I will get some things wrong because I still must learn about each child. But despite all the mistakes I will make, I hope they realize that my mistakes were out of an effort to lessen the impact of life's blows on each of them. If I told my kids that only I can choose their path in life and that they are nothing without me, you would probably think I was a monster, right? What kind of a loving father has as his goal to make his kids feel inferior, so they only depend on him?

I would like to think that Jesus did not come to make us feel inferior to God, but to remind us that we are gods within the domain of our lives. It makes sense that Jesus had to be cryptic about freedom, given the blood thirsty disposition of those in power during his time. But even if God does control everything, what kind of "free spirit" is there to be if the power to control our own thoughts and behavior is not one of the qualities inherent to our essence? What kind of spiritual freedom is there to have, if not the freedom to responsibly create or pursue the life we want to live? Is it God's will that we must not act by our own accord or is this the will of the "devil" to turn us into spirits without willpower? I could go on and on, but I am sure you get the point.

If what defines you strips you of the essential qualities that form the foundation of life, you will see yourself only as a mortal being. Therefore, the possibility of life before birth will be strange to you, unless you are a free spirit. To be clear, when I say "free spirit" I hope you don't get the idea that I am talking about the Hippie version. Not at all. That is the humanized version of freedom. What I mean by free spirit is just that, a free spirit, as in, you are aware of what you are, and therefore not tangled or confused with what you are not. If you can then design and live your life in a way that keeps your trinity balanced, while doing your part to help maintain life's balance, you are free. Freedom does not imply that we are liberated from responsibility. On the contrary, our ability to take responsibility is what makes freedom possible. All that responsibility amounts to, is being able to embrace what you are, being able to tend to your trinity's needs, and being willing to help others and life in general when you can.

In essence, we are spirits with a human alter ego. If we depend on form-based logic only to define ourselves, we will substitute our timeless qualities with something artificial. Our earthly derived convictions will become the blind spots that will allow our human alter ego to become the dominant entity. This is why our spiritual freedom depends on our ability and willingness to undo the conclusions that keep us subservient to our human alter egos. That is why reevaluating how we define ourselves is essential in our pursuit of spiritual freedom. Otherwise, we are destined to trap ourselves through a framework of thinking that does not accommodate our intrinsic state of existence. This can make it harder for us to step back and be ourselves without feeling conflicted about which one is our truest identity. I hope this helps to broaden your perspective so that you can see beyond the façade of our human existence.

THE SPIRITUAL TRUTH THAT TIME OBSCURES

Do you ever feel like you remain still while time goes by? This is a fascinating experience that I first noticed during an out-of-body experience. I was conscious, yet not attached to my body. My connection to time was simply my awareness of the present. And my body was like a proxy in time. I became very curious about the workings of time since then. But it was not until recently that I realized that time itself depends on conscious activity to exist. I will admit, it's impossible to see that from a human perspective. Of course, our bodies and state of mind can change through time. But do you, the observer really change, or it's *what* you are observing that's changing? This right here, is the stuff of Zen, as in meditation. The significance of time boils down to how *you* define yourself.

This brings me to the 2,500-year-old story about an Indian prince who gave up his royal life to seek enlightenment in the hopes of ending human suffering. We know him today as the Buddha, the enlightened one.

I will not bore you by trying to tell you the story of the Buddha. I will leave that for those who are qualified to tell his story more compellingly than I can. However, there is a fundamental value that his story highlights quite well. But make no mistake, that value is not unique to Siddhartha Gautama. It is said by those who tell the story of the Buddha that he found enlightenment sitting under a tree. That was only after he was able to take a "step back" from the noise of life and his own mind. The story of the Buddha highlights the value of being able to take a step back from the noise of our material existence, to open ourselves to deeper insights into the essence of existence.

I first got a glimpse into meditation from my great grandmother. She used to sit under a tree for hours in deep thought, using a straw of dry grass as a toothpick. Her wisdom helped me start to piece together spirituality way before I knew anything about Buddhism. I must confess, seeing her in that state made me uncomfortable, since I was one of those kids with so much energy! The thought of sitting for that long was excruciating to me. So, I would occasionally impishly skip along to where she was sitting and poke the hornet's nest, just to see what was going on with her. Lucky for me, she was not very quick to anger. But she would occasionally snarl at me unexpectedly, which scared the living daylights out of me!

Looking back, I think part of the reason why I was so hyper was because I was trying to keep myself distracted from having to contemplate the mysteries of life that I was beginning to question. Consequently, me being "all over the place" was an outward manifestation of the fact that I did not have any format or way to process my curiosity of life freely and in a meaningful way. This has now changed since I've learned the value of being able to ask a question, observe life, and then simply let the revelations unfold; then repeat that process until I find the core answer or truth.

Anyway, back to the subject at hand, we often lose ourselves within the changes of time as we grow up and become preoccupied with the hectic business of survival. The more focused we get on only surviving, the more intertwined we become with time. So, we forget that time exists primarily as part of our collective conscious activities. This is not something that I just conjured up. History is littered with examples of how even as mankind, we've shaped the course of time for better or for worse. Regardless of whether you view time from an individual perspective, or from the origins of the universe, you cannot have a sense of time unless you designate where it begins, where it is now, and the future. So, if the existence of time depends on having an **observer**, *what then is the nature of the observer before time?* Careful not to jump to conclusions on this one!

There is a fundamental condition that must be true for heaven or hell to be real. That condition is we must have a natural capacity to live beyond our physical death. In other words, we must be immortal. This suggests that heaven or hell can't exist if we are only human. But if we are immortal, this also suggests that immortality fundamentally has two main extremes, heaven being the most ideal and hell being, well—hellish. For as long as I can remember in my Christian upbringing, I've had a lingering question about how a spirit, a formless entity could burn in hell. It's quite a dilemma if you think about it. But it's most likely that my question was an inevitable enigma from the time when I took the Bible too literal.

We can trace the origins of the concept of hell to the sinister history of the Valley of Hinnom, also known as Gehinnom or Gehenna, located south of the ancient City of Jerusalem. To give you a brief overview, the Valley of Hinnom was the place where the children of Judah exercised the horrific practice of passing their children through fire as a sacrifice to the pagan god Moloch. The Hinnom Valley also became a city dump for garbage and ghastly remains of animals and humans alike. In Biblical times, the Hinnom Valley was set on fire to get rid of the garbage and all else that was there. It seemed like that fire burned endlessly, ergo, hell!

As far as I understand, the Bible references the Hinnom Valley metaphorically to draw a parallel of the consequences that await those who were set on a life of sin[2]. But to me, it seems unfitting for a God of love to be so punitive as to cast his own children in a lake of fire, like those who made such sacrifices to Moloch. This is why I find it hard to believe in the widely accepted concept of hell. However, I have no doubt that hell like suffering is real, even for immortal beings.

If you wanted to live with a free conscience and you had to choose between gods that normalized cruelty by requiring sacrifices and the God of love, I am sure you would find that there

---

[2] See Mark 9:43–47, New Testament for Everyone (NTE)

is one obvious choice that fits in with the lifestyle of having a free conscience.

Heaven and hell represent the dual nature of life. They are a visual contrast of the realities of joy and pain; peace and war; or freedom and captivity. What the history of the Hinnom Valley teaches us is that there is a point of no return in the choices that we make. I don't know anyone that can sacrifice their child for the sake of wealth and still retain their humanity. I don't know of anyone that is unable to feel remorse for their harmful actions and still be reformed. I don't know of any healthy relationship in which there can be no trust. Thus, the point of no return is the point at which something spoils and takes on less desirable qualities. Not to be grim here, but for humanity, nuclear war would be such a point.

The power to make a choice is our most consequential power. Yet sometimes we can be too casual with this power to our own detriment. The presence or absence of a choice is the heart of individual freedom or lack of freedom. But an even more fundamental power to the power of choice, is knowledge or enlightenment. So yes, the adage that "knowledge is power" is very true! Because without knowledge, we have little to no insight about the consequences of our choices, unlike when we take necessary risks, like choosing to fight for freedom against tyranny. This is why children are not free technically, until they know enough to navigate life by themselves.

Like any other form of power, there are natural consequences to abusing our power of choice in a way that violates life's natural order or the core of our individuality. It's vital that we understand this because behind any human caused tragedy, such as the tragedies of the Hinnom Valley or war, and so on, you will find suppression, corruption, exploitation, or selfish use of the power of choice. Tyranny robs the people of their power of choice. Ignorance diminishes or erodes the power of choice. Lies seek to exploit the power of choice and so on. Crime, on the other hand, suggests a selfish use of the power of choice in a way that is harmful. So, this forces society to create a system to address those who bring harm to others due to an inability to control their actions in extreme cases. In such a case, the individual's lack of self-control is a point of no return that then justifies intervention from other members of society.

As for spiritual beings, there is a point of no return at which we become alienated from our essence beyond our ability to freely exist. And from that point, we relinquish our independence and any potential that is native to us. This creates a vacuum of awareness about our fundamental qualities or our true potential. As a result, we become more dependent on form to define our existence, and the rest is history! Once we forget what we are, time steps in and takes over as the natural law that governs all form. Hence, we find ourselves destined to cease to exist once we are oblivious of our true nature. So, oblivion becomes our point of no return as spiritual beings.

The point of no return is a natural law as far as I can tell. We know this to be true instinctively, that is why we feel compelled to cut ties with people whom we cannot trust, or people who always try to tear us down for no good reason, right? If you cut someone off from the privilege of your company justifiably, are you to take the blame for defending your individuality or sanity? If the answer is no, then in the grand scheme of things, we cannot lay the responsibility for any eternal suffering at God's feet. This is why I think heaven and hell are allegories for two of our potential spiritual conditions, whether desirable or undesirable.

Ironically, we cannot find spiritual redemption without owning up to our mistakes in the same way that we would expect anyone who wrongs us to show remorse for their actions, and take steps to ensure that they don't cross that line again. In other words, we must seek to understand how we have gone past the "point of no return" and remedy that. This can be hard to do without any empathy, love, or support from others. Because past the point of no return, spiritually, we must depend on better examples of what we could be from others.

Fortunately, we are able to figure out the mistakes that led to our spiritual demise through the help of the enlightened beings who have walked the earth throughout history. We can argue about what is meant by heaven and hell, but unless you understand what these words symbolize within the context of a spiritual point of no return, you might not see that the path towards your revival begins with you defining yourself in the truest possible sense. Only then will you gain the tenacity to outgrow the lies that diminished your awareness and kept you captive.

Due to history's portrayal of brutal religious practices like penance, some people only see religion as a mechanism for obedience. However, religion or any form of true spirituality must be a mechanism for enlightening and reawakening the spirit to its eternal existence. Spirituality should serve to remind us not to become consumed by or parish with time, while living in human form.

When you rediscover your essence free of form, you will realize that you as a spiritual being can exist within or outside of the context of time. If you can embrace that realization, it will also restore your awareness of the fact that your existence is not bound by or defined by time. That to me is spiritual freedom!

Some say that time is a cruel master. There is some truth to this because time does force us to relive our mistakes, until we are mature in mind and in spirit. All the powerful spiritual wisdom in this world means nothing with no one to wield it. No smart map or GPS system can benefit anyone that is not willing to travel. What this means is spiritual awakening is a path that you must be willing to walk before the truth can serve you. Jesus alludes to our spiritual responsibility in Matthew 16:24–26 paraphrased, when he told his disciples to "take up their own cross and follow him." By following him I don't think he meant for his disciples to cling on to every word he said in poetic awe. But that they must take ownership for their spiritual shortcomings and seek the truth to find spiritual redemption. To me, taking responsibility for our spiritual missteps is the most logical meaning behind the metaphor of taking up our crosses. And time could very well be one of our biggest crosses to bear.

Let me explain. Time is essentially part of our conscious faculties that serve to classify the sequence of events from a reasonable starting point to the present, in order to predict or decide the future. The ability to set things in motion with a predictable outcome and to solve problems thereof are the essence of intelligence. And behind intelligence we can find the causation, intention, or purpose behind the happenings or events that we call time. This concept is not easy to grasp when we define ourselves as form, which exist only within the context of time. Therefore, we must try to take a step back and look at time as conscious beings to see how our conscious activity and force of purpose impacts events, in other words time.

For example, if a driver steps into a car and sets it in motion, that driver has the responsibility to keep their eyes on the road and do their best to navigate any obstacles to reach their intended destination. However, if that driver decides to sit back with their arms folded while the car is going, we can all see that there will be a predictable outcome. Such is our responsibility to bear with life as spiritual beings living in this time collective.

Time is a system that gives us reference points that help us navigate life as form. Nevertheless, if we don't consider our consciousness as the prime reference point from which the journey of life begins on a *path* of *purpose*, we will lose our true north. We cannot find our way back *home* (to our prime nature), without knowing what home is to begin with. We become the lost ones in the sea of time and life forms if we forget our true nature. I think this is what Jesus meant according to John 8:14 when he told the Pharisees, "Even if I bear witness of myself, my witness is true for I know where I come from and where I am going." John

8 reveals that Jesus did not think of himself as bound within the confines of time. He saw things from a point before the beginning of time, whereas the Pharisees only thought of their origins within the parameters of time. This explains why the Pharisees had a hard time understanding Jesus.

I hope you will not mistake my quoting the Bible as an effort to impose my religious views. It is not. But I must say there is quite a bit of spiritual truths that we can distil from the Bible without requiring any blind faith to understand it. When it comes to spirituality, my heart is set on the truth above all else. Why? Because without the truth, we lack the *timeless* affirmations of our essence, and therefore we will have no power to transcend beyond the grip of time. I don't believe that the truth is something that can be forced on people, as some try to do. Because truth implies that your understanding of it is part of the truth. So, once you see the truth, you will willingly embrace the truth as it elevates your awareness of your core *timeless* qualities. Jesus understood that the truth cannot be forced on people. That is why he was a teacher, not a dictator of truth.

Spirituality is not an argument for God, since to argue for God, we must presume to know God. That's a tall order to fill, even for the most God-fearing man or woman! However, you don't have to presume that you are a conscious being. Therefore, spirituality is an argument that we are spiritual beings at the core, based on a healthy skepticism that there are things evolution alone cannot account for, like how something as purposeful as DNA came into being, without any purpose driven conscious activity. So, for me, my fascination with religion began through my effort to understand my intrinsic nature, nothing more. To say otherwise would be a lie!

I don't know about you, but one of the things that I did not learn in church is that you and I are part of the truth of life. This can make it difficult to reconcile ourselves with our true nature because (to use a popular term) we can cancel ourselves from being part of the truth through our beliefs. This makes the noise of time even more effective at hiding our essence, because we cancel ourselves out of existence first before we can give time the power to *obscure* our existence.

Time is such a mind-bending mystery when we live under the conviction that we are only of this world. We turn off our awareness from any faint suspicions that suggest we are not part of time. As a result, we grow accustomed to setting our default sense of identity based on *form*. The issue here is not our interaction with timely forms. There is nothing wrong with having form. The story of Jesus illustrates that we can live in form and not be consumed by it as he did. However, if we submit to the conviction that we are only of this world, time will dictate what we are, and the scope of our awareness. And that is how we allow time to keep us from realizing our eternal selves. This is a recipe for hell as far as I understand.

So, how do we begin to verify our spiritual qualities? I find that silent contemplation is a potent catalyst for me. I know that silence can be uncomfortable, since silence feels like we are cutting ties with the world. Nevertheless, we must find the courage to embrace silence with the purpose of amplifying our awareness. The Buddhist have their finger on the money with the practice of meditation. But if the purpose of meditation is not clearly defined, meditation can turn into spiritually unnourishing escapism.

I think the most powerful use of meditation is using it to isolate or pull ourselves away from the noise of living, so that we can get a better view of life, and therefore better insights. Sometimes it is hard to resist our urge to participate in time, just like it might be hard for you to resist tapping your foot or dancing when a pleasing song is playing. But if you can resist the pull of time and simply be its witness, you may gradually start to amplify your essence as the conscious observer. If you can safely take a step back, and simply observe time with the understanding that your awareness brings time to life, you will find a clarity, serenity, and bliss that is out of this world!

If you were to imagine yourself alone in a forest, you will find that your awareness sustains your existence. Realize that your existence and individuality depend on that primary awareness above all else. Your existence is not dependent on others being aware of you. But your *relationship* with others depends on your awareness of them and their mutual awareness of you. I think our relationships will work much better when we all have a fundamental awareness of ourselves and a respect for each other's individuality.

If there is a heaven, I believe that it is a state of awareness above the chaos of time. Heaven should exist outside of time as part of the eternal, right? So, what makes us think that heaven is not within our reach at any moment? Is it possible that we cannot experience heaven because we think of it as only existing in the future? Can the way that we define ourselves limit our awareness so that we lose the ability to experience heaven?

Well, these are questions that only you can find answers to through meditation and revelations. Happiness is inner beauty captured in the form of an emotion. When you find and embrace the answers that reflect the beauty of your essence, you will experience the serenity or inner beauty that is happiness.

LIFE BEFORE FORM

N ow that we've looked at examples of areas of conclusions that can impede our ability to explore and grasp the formless nature of life, I hope that we can now unpack this *vital* aspect of life from a perspective that is not confined by time or our human existence. The question of life before birth has been staring me in the face for a long time. It is one of the most elusive subjects to convey in plain English without drawing a contrast between our transient existence versus our eternal nature. Everything finally came together for me while I was writing a short article on how time obscures our spiritual nature. I realized that I was looking at spirituality from two perspectives that were too far in the sequence of events regarding our human lives, and these are conception and death.

It dawned on me that the entire pursuit of spiritual salvation is illogical without considering life before conception. Because it is the quest of the essence that we once knew ourselves to be (before we took form), that makes the foundation of spirituality. In life, we are sometimes taught to avoid looking at the past under the generalized assumption that the past only bears pain. Well, that is not the case with spirituality. To understand how we got here, we must look at the past, as in how we got involved with time and form to begin with. Unless we realize that something with the potential of life exists, before life takes form, we will not see that life begins and "ends" at the same formless point. But if you can see that life begins and ends in a formless state, not nothingness, you will also realize that time and identity are part of the transient illusions of our human existence.

I wouldn't be so naïve to think that man has successfully resisted the temptation to alter the Bible for the sake of power. Some of the most influential cult leaders and false prophets are known to name-drop God, to keep believers oblivious of their intentions. I also have my qualms with how the Bible was translated to make Jesus sound like a 15th century bard, and what may have been lost in translation in trying to fit his teachings to the poetic cultural phenomena of that time. So, for those reasons, I reserve my right to be skeptical. However, something occasionally stands out for me from the Bible in a way that I can only think of as a subtle affirmation. One verse that comes to mind about life before form is Jeremiah 1:5, and it reads, "Before I formed you in the womb I *knew* you, and before you were born, I consecrated you; I appointed you a prophet to the nations." Just meditate on this for a moment.

I don't know what your thoughts are on God, Jesus, or the Bible, but when it comes to hints or clues as to the potential of life before birth, Jeremiah 1:5 is a bombshell of a clue! Not only that, Jesus in his largely misunderstood parables and teachings left many hints and clues to awaken us to the phenomena of life before birth. In fact, the theme of Jesus' life begins and ends back in a formless state. This is the point that I think his life meant to illuminate. So, if you follow him by his purpose for living, you will understand where he was leading us, not as human beings, but as spiritual beings lost in time and form.

Outside of the Bible, my great grandmother used to tell me that it was part of our cultural beliefs that the spirit affectionately lingers around an expectant mother to try and win her favor. So, when I look at all this in addition to the moment when I found myself in a formless state, the purpose of spirituality is clear! Spirituality is not a fad. It is something necessary to keep you and me spiritually and mentally free to navigate life without getting lost in it. Therefore, to me, the ultimate test of a life well lived is whether we can return to the point where it all started.

Understanding and recognizing the existence of the spirit before the spirit takes form must be an integral part of spirituality. Otherwise, the foundation and purpose of spirituality will be null! Why? Because there will be nothing to redeem! If we neglect our natural existence before form, we will erase all there is to know about our nature, our true potentials, and our abilities. This is what eventually makes us become dependent on the history of form to get a sense of identity. The idea that we are just "blank slates" when we are born is misleading. Because it implies that there is nothing to know, leaving us empty and oblivious of the truth that *essential* to human lives, it's the spirit that possesses the potential to give life to form. So, we got where we are now giving life to our human form, and somehow, we ended up thinking that form is all there is to life.

I have no doubt that there are environmental factors that can limit our spiritual potential as well. Let's take a child for example, what makes it possible to take a child from any race in the world, move them in with a different race, and they can create an identity in every way independent of form, based on their new environment? This tells us that our cultural identity is not native to us. It's something that we learn! So, we can inherit the freedoms and limitations native to the culture we live in. But occasionally, something from the outside ignites our forgotten potential, like music, and makes us dream beyond our environmentally or culturally indoctrinated limitations.

Similarly, in life we may encounter experiences that lift us from the entrenchment of our human existence. And in that moment, we can see beyond the façade of our human existence. Therefore, we dare to dream that there must be something more to life than this transient form. However, we are constantly indoctrinated to feel ashamed of even considering the possibility. Some might go as far as thinking that it is irrational to think of life outside the context of form. But I assure you, those are the opinions of those who are spiritually oblivious. So, don't let their oblivion convince you otherwise. Because some of the most difficult blind spots that will make you doubt your spiritual nature, are your own conclusions. To make matters worse, if you did not know that the conclusions you make can be true, false, or somewhere in between, you will have no freedom to take a step back from them and see how they affect your awareness. And that is why the Spectrum of Conclusions Chart is a valuable tool for any truth seeker.

What thrills me most about the revelation of life before form is that we don't have to only look at spirituality through the eyes of death, as we often do based on our religious persuasions. Rather, I find that embracing spirituality from the perspective of *life before form* feels more natural, since it explains how the hereafter is an actuality, not just a figment of our imagination. Whether you will be aware or not of your essence in the hereafter is a separate matter. That will depend on whether you can comfortably distinguish yourself from the form you possess, and whether you can *master* and embrace your own essence despite of living in human form.

From a human perspective, it is impossible to fully appreciate our immortality or to understand that we are lost in this world, without having anyone who exemplifies our truest qualities. So, we are fortunate that history affords us the luxury to look back at the lives of spiritual teachers like Jesus, the Buddha, or whomever it may be for your case, who left some clues to enlighten us about our true nature. Nevertheless, regardless of what our personal beliefs may be, it seems to me that our spiritual freedom can only become a reality if we can return to the state where our nature is pure and where we are vibrantly conscious of our existence as spiritual beings.

When I first heard that Buddhism was about ending the cycle of birth and death, I used to think that it was quite audacious of the Buddha to think so. But, as I peel away my own layers of spiritual misconceptions, I realize my rejection of the notion that death could be ended was based on what I did not know about my ultimate nature of existence. This is humbling in a good way. My approach to spirituality is quite simple now. I don't look for the truth in the context of religion. Instead, I look for the truth by opening myself to experience the uniform indispensable qualities of life. Because the truth of life must ultimately be consistent with existence, not religion.

There so much that we don't know or that remains buried away behind the fog of our form-based reality and fear driven belief systems. Sometimes it's difficult to pull ourselves out of that fog due to our tendency to prefer our comfort zone over the truth. And sometimes our fear of the unseen distorts our ability to perceive our fundamental nature. So, in a nutshell, the truth may remain hidden right under our noses because of conclusions that limit our ability to consider and experience life for what it is!

As we are discussing life before birth, I must also clarify that I do not mean this in the sense of past lives. This is not to negate any validity to anyone who recalls having a past life. However, pursuing past lives keeps us dependent on time for spiritual affirmation. The way I see it, the goal of spirituality is for us to awaken to what we were before we became dependent on time and form for existence. Time exists primarily in contrast to something timeless. This tells me that we cannot grasp immortality by looking for it inside of time, as is the case with past lives. So, this sets the bar very high on what I mean when I talk about life before birth. While anyone that recalls their past life witnesses a *remarkable* spiritual anomaly, that experience may not always translate outside of time and form without an understanding of what it is about us that makes past lives possible. For that reason, understanding the core of what we are is what takes anyone's experience of a past life from being a mystery, to being a spiritual affirmation.

Theoretical physicists scratch their heads when they strip form from the universe, down to the fabric of space. From what I understand, what they have found so far is that space is not nothing. But what fascinates me the most about their theorizing, is that they seem to think very little about the role of the observer of space, to the fundamental existence of space. To me, the greatest mystery is not space, but the nature of the observer. Since, even when we theoretically remove all form down to the core of space, at least two things must remain, that is, the fabric of space and its observer! So here again, we find ourselves in a "which came first, the chicken or the egg" type of situation. The bottom line is, unless we suspect that there is a *third* factor that keeps illuding our awareness, we cannot take a step back and solve this binary riddle of space. But with the concept of the trinity, we learn that there must be at least three factors, not two, in any instance of existence. That third factor could be the potential or purpose of the observer.

I think most spiritual people must be crude theoretical physicists to some degree. Because we also strip life down to almost nothing and then we realize, nope, there must be something more to the story of life. As a result, spirituality picks things up past the limitations of theoretical physics, which is a form-based science, and tries to illuminate the essence of the mysterious observer that physicists treat as an afterthought. And the benefit that we gain from all the rigorous research that has led physicists to the material of space, is the understanding that form does not define the essence of existence.

In a way, theoretical physicists may have unintentionally affirmed the actuality of life before form when they reduce the universe down to space. How? Because they themselves must also have no form as they remove all things from the universe to study the nature of space. The only thing that is indispensable in their study of space, is the formless and intelligent observer that they themselves must remain as, to still study the essence of space.

Don't get me wrong, I have high respect for theoretical physicists, and I have no doubt that they are smart people. But the fact that they don't suspect at all if the observer has anything to do with the existence of space can put them in a situation like that of a dog chasing its own tail, if you will. If they assume or conclude that the observer has nothing to do with the phenomena of space, the nature of space will remain a mystery. This again illustrates how a premature conclusion can limit our awareness. I often think of space as a three-dimensional canvas on which the spirit projects what is to be and then takes steps to manifests what is to be. Sometimes we get so involved in the process of living that we fail to realize how our conscious activity is an integral part of life. While I put theoretical physicists on the spot here, we all have a similar blind spot to some degree when we take on the question of existence. Let this settle in before you move on.

If you look at human existence the same way theoretical physicists are studying space, you will find that at least consciousness, potential, and our ability to enact our potential or decide to act remains. This gives us a point of access into the purpose of form and a sense of the vital force or drive that is native to the spirit. You may have already suspected what the fundamental nature of life is, but you might also have had your doubts about it like I did. What I realized is that most of my doubts had to do with the fact that I was carrying over logic and laws that affect form, like time for instance, and then tried to impose that logic on the formless. I am sure you can see how that can be a problem. Form-based logic is the dominant logic of our human survival. That is why we cannot easily conceptualize the essence of life without form, unless we step out of the zone of form-driven logic.

When you look at the fact that consciousness and intelligence are indispensable to the study of time, space, form, or formless existence, you may start to see what our natural state of existence *is* before we become intertwined with form and its predictable destiny. Therefore, it is my belief that our individual rediscovery of our original state is what sets us spiritually free. Can you imagine the relief and bliss that such an affirmed realization can bring? I believe that the reason why we find the concept of heaven quite appealing is because it does closely approximate our natural instincts about our eternal nature. The concept of heaven keeps us connected to what we instinctively know about our transcendent nature. That is why the belief in heaven has lived through time in many forms, from nirvana to paradise.

When we understand life from the perspective that we already exist and simply adopt form to serve our purpose, death ceases to be a sentence to non-existence. Accordingly, as we become less dependent on time and form to define ourselves, time and form will lose the power to obscure our eternal nature.

THE PROSPECTS OF IMMORTALITY

Mankind has dreamt of immortality for as long as recorded history tells us, and probably beyond. Many have searched for immortality. Some may have found the secrets to immortality through enlightenment. Others might have grown weary of the prospects of their own immortality, blinded by the notion that existence only implies the presence of form. Whether we can understand immortality or regard it as a pipe dream depends on the premise from which we view immortality. Naturally, dreaming of immortality as human is not the best premise from which to explore the prospects of immortality. I know that if I did not have any experiences that awakened me to my spiritual nature, I too would have been skeptical about immortality. Thankfully, because of my experiences, I now see that immortality can only be part of our spiritual nature, whether we are aware of it or not.

It's safe to say that those who can embrace the hope of immortality with ease are the ones who have known somehow that they are guests in this world. But even such hope can sometimes fade away as we gradually become corrupted by the Trojan horse of humanized spirituality. So as our perspective gradually shifts from the essence of our spiritual nature and gets tangled with human existence, we might also become eclipsed from the immortality that is inherent to our nature.

Some believe that immortality is something that we are granted by God after death. Given what we have covered, would you say such a notion stems from an understanding of our true nature, or is this notion based on the conviction that we are *only* human? The way I see it, if we believe that life begins at conception, it makes sense that we would also believe that immortality only exists after death. But what do we suppose we will exist as, if we did not already exist before birth? A ghostly form of our human life, I suppose. So, from this narrative, immortality can't be intrinsic to us, can you see? This suggests that something must perpetually create us in time as ghostly forms of our human existence, or maybe as an idol of some sort. I don't know about you, but that does not sound like immortality to me.

The truth about immortality cannot come full circle unless it's also true that we existed before birth and before time. This means you have no past to revisit, except your true nature. You have no present outside of your current trinity. And you have no future besides what you create. This tells me that immortality has to do with our ability to discern, affirm, and simply embrace our core nature outside of all that is created, including our human form. As far as I know, it's only when we try to *equate* ourselves with form that we begin to overthink immortality, rather than realize that it is *simply* part of our nature.

Whenever we have tried to humanize spiritual concepts, we end up with an inferior version of spirituality. Immortality is not immune to such degraded spirituality. We've got everything from mummies, bronze, stone, and wooden statues that immortalize form and suggest to us a lifeless form of immortality, not to forget wax museums. So, all we can hope for is that we will be seared into the minds of the world and our loved ones through imagery. The only problem with such a frozen piece of time is it could also lead us to conclude that we too will become a frozen piece of time someday. This of course goes against our true nature. So, once we erase the awareness that gives us the footing to exist outside of time, we give time the power to decide our existence. Good luck trying to understand immortality after that!

If we cannot trace our steps back to our true nature, the promise of immortality will remain a fantastic proposal. It's even harder to believe in life after death if we cannot see ourselves existing before conception. Death does not transform us into spiritual beings. Let this sink in for a moment! We are spiritual beings first and foremost, before we take up any form. When we understand that life is a manifestation of spirit, purpose, and form existing as one entity, we can also see that death is nothing more than a decoupling of that trinity. During that process, it is my belief that the spirit can become *displaced,* having swapped its core attributes with form. Therefore, in that displaced condition, the potential for its non-existence feels as real as void space.

Romans 6:23, paraphrased, tells us "The wage of sin is death." That doesn't make much sense when you consider the fact that the unborn still die even before living a life of sin. This tells us that sin must mean something else beyond the muddy story of Adam and Eve or moral delinquency. Accordingly, death must also mean something else to be a wage of sin that children are exempt from, right? Besides, hell cannot be real if death is absolute. Think about that for a moment. This is where Theology gets a bit muddy! However, we can still derive from the Bible that as spiritual beings, we have embraced a way of being that is *not* true to our nature, therefore a lie. That lie must have been the beginning of our downward spiral, and we've been lost ever since.

One part of the Bible that makes me wonder if Jesus said a lot more about our immortality than what the Bible tells us is Psalms 82:5–7, in which he supposedly said, "They know not, neither will they understand; they walk on in darkness: all the foundations of the earth are out of course. I have said, you are gods; and all of you are children of the most High. *But* you shall die like men, and fall like one of the princes." Was he suggesting that we only die *like* man because we forgot that we are gods? By the way these were Jesus' words, according to Psalms 82, not mine. This begs the question, could our original transgression be that we deviated from our true nature? It certainly makes sense in this context. Because in thinking of our existence only in human form, we degrade ourselves to mortal beings. Only then can we become estranged from our immortality.

Some Christians are quite uncomfortable with Psalms 82, as if they deem themselves unworthy of being likened to God or something. Honestly, I get it! Christian or not, it can be overwhelming to think that we have such big shoes to fill. But could that be because we define ourselves only as human, so we cannot embrace the essence of godliness present within the fact of our *living*?

We cannot see the reflection of God's nature in ourselves while embracing the conviction that we are only human! And that is the problem! As such, we cannot rise above human limitations. But since we now understand the problem, I hope that we can start taking baby steps towards the full revival of our core nature. Hopefully, we can also recover any potential that we had to disown to fit in with only being humans.

If we look deeper into life, existence implies an awareness of the act or condition of existing! So, awareness is indispensable from existence. This tells us that for the spirit, death must begin with the conclusion that there is nothing to be aware of without form. That is exactly what the denial of our true nature accomplishes. From that point, it is perfectly logical for us to conclude that we cannot exist without form, so we succumb to time. But to be convinced that the spirit dies, we must erase any trace of ourselves. That means we must also *hide*, even from ourselves! Well, I can't think of a better place to hide than behind the shadows of time. Fittingly, as time continues to obscure our true essence beyond our grasp, we find ourselves in oblivion. Nonetheless, as the saying goes, "the truth always comes out." Well, I can't argue with that, especially when that truth involves something paramount to existence!

It takes a lot of energy to hide being someone's secret Santa for a few days. Imagine how much energy you will need to invest to become oblivious of your eternal nature! Someone will read this and go "huh?" Exactly my point! We have had to act clueless for so long under the veil of form and time to a point where the hardest thing for us to do, is being our true selves! So, unless we become equally committed to undoing any premise, conclusions, or choices that led us here, we will continue to give up our power beyond the point of no return! It is fitting that Karma would gradually take over as a natural consequence as we continue to neglect, give up, or abuse our inherent power.

I am fully aware that there is quite a bit of superstition about what Karma is exactly. But as far as I know, the concept of Karma is as simple as saying there are consequences for breaking the law. Except with Karma, we are dealing with natural laws or life's natural order. Karma is the unpredictability of life that follows when we make any choice that is detrimental to our fundamental nature, thus impairing our ability to keep our life in order. From that point, we could cause harm to ourselves and others by nature of losing control. Going against life's natural order or laws brings about undesirable consequences, the least being diminishing our freedom or power to act.

To put things in perspective, if someone chooses to drink and drive, everything is up to chance the moment they step into the car drunk. To be clear, it's at the point that such a driver has no conscious control of their car when things get more unpredictable than usual. When things become dangerously unpredictable, we expect only bad things to happen. And that is Karma. So, luck is what we call any good that comes out of such an unpredictable situation. Whatever forces take over when we are no longer in control decide the outcome. If you are in control, things are predictable. You decide the outcome, not by forcing things, but by understanding and working with the nature of things. In such a case, you are in control, which is the opposite of Karma.

From a spiritual perspective, when we are not cognizant of our true nature, we are in a situation where much of our potential is out of our reach as we subconsciously persecute ourselves. While every individual is different, what is clear is that we cannot access our potential when we believe in lies that obscure our true nature! Since life is already happening, the *impetus* of time serves as karma. I believe this is why Jesus said "they walk in darkness: all the foundations of the earth are out of course" in Psalms 82, referring to mankind. If you understand this, then you can also see what we must do to restore order to our world.

I propose that an atheist is simply someone that has inverted from their own true nature. Their rejection of any notion of God (a formless entity with the potential to create *and* bring **form** to life), is based on a fundamental rejection of their own essence, if not simply a protest of religious overreach. Since by denying the spiritual origins of life, they nullify themselves as spiritual beings. So, they cannot see the possibility of life before form! As a result, evolution becomes the plateau of reason that they must assume to make sense of life. But try as they may, they can't deny the spirit out of existence. So, they hide behind a self-deprecating premise that helps to keep them oblivious of themselves. However, to live at all, they must still imbue their lives with purpose, goals, or dreams, which are higher functions they cannot fully account for through evolution.

We face nothing but self-imposed limitations when we define our primal nature only within the parameters of form, be it in the context of our DNA, race, or gender. Because form is limited by nature. It may sound smart for us to attribute all that we do not understand about ourselves to "complex brain function." But that would be as unsound as a pilot thinking only the cockpit defines who they are! So, unless we realize that our primal nature is fundamentally formless and refined, we will not understand why we aspire to be rational, why we enjoy harmony over chaos, or why we dream of heaven as the destiny for divinely redeemed souls. Therefore, the premise that we choose to define ourselves within can precipitate our spiritual redemption or demise. Given all that we have covered, I am sure you can figure out which premise of life has a point of no return inherent to it for any spiritual being that embraces it.

If there is a devil at all, it would be one who tempts or tricks you out of your true nature. Not necessarily a beastly humanoid creature with hooves for feet, a tail, and some horns. When we look at the stories in the Bible as anecdotal analogies of how we fell from our godlike nature, everything starts to make sense! However, if we think of everything in the Bible as literal, we will miss the spiritual teachings behind the proverbs. If anything, the messaging in the Bible was meant to meet us where we are (being humans), while reminding us that we are more than just human.

The word sinner can come across as an insult to some, a mark of guilt for some or a badge of notoriety for the renegade. It serves no good to simply regard everyone as a sinner without knowing what sin is to begin with. Therefore, we must demystify sin in a way that an individual can relate to within themselves before they can be willing to participate in saving themselves. If we look at the nature of sin without any puritan or religious undertones, we can see that it simply means a destructive decision or choice that leads to destructive or evil actions. Given that the spirit bears the responsibility of keeping its domain of life copacetic, what could be more destructive than the decision to abnegate its true nature?

The moral teachings of the Bible address us at a human level. And while morals may help us fight our self-destructive urges, we can become aloof to them over time if they are not supported by an understanding of our core nature, followed by spiritual rehabilitation. Morality by itself cannot vanquish what ails the spirit. And what ails the spirit in my observation, is the misidentification of itself. So, it follows that when we apply morals to ourselves, yet not understand or see a path to return to our fundamental nature, the root of our misdeeds will remain! As a result, we will relapse into our comfort zone or our addiction with only form driven incentives or value.

Today, the world faces moral challenges that indicate we have work to do before we can free ourselves and reclaim our power from the grip of our form self-indulgences. Religious leaders find themselves dealing with an invisible ailment that they do not understand. We have seen men and women of morals turn to politics to enact laws to "fix" what they believe is only moral depravity. But what they do not realize is that morality is merely a tourniquet for what ails the spirit. A fickle one at that! The spirit is resilient, even when oblivious of itself. Therefore, its self-destructive habits will persist along with it, unless given the enlightenment and power to save itself.

For any relationship to function, whether it's between individuals, cultures, or nations, there must be some natural and mutually valued ideals to facilitate fair or amenable interactions. The inherent function of morals is to sustain healthy relationships between individuals, cultures, or nations. What morals cannot do, is fix what's broken within an individual, yet some people insist that lack of morality is the problem with mankind. As far as I can tell, the absence of morality is not the problem, but it's a symptom of spiritual impairment or lack of self-awareness that leads to the repression of one's rational faculties.

Trying to enforce extrinsic or arbitrary values as "morals" only creates or excites rebels. Such morals, if we should call them that, often make individuals bitter about morality. If the function of morality is to support fair interactions or facilitate our coexistence, any moral system that takes away from those goals lacks the function value that we must expect from a viable moral system. History teaches us that any system of laws that neglect an individual's sovereignty is not naturally sustainable. Likewise, a flawed moral system can become too irrational to be sustainable over time. Consequently, such a system causes chaos as it fails to establish the mechanisms for accord that are essential for healthy relationships to exist.

We cannot experience true reform unless we can learn to take responsibility for our mistakes and aspire to reasonably self-govern. If morality is about being obedient to a higher power, we must first convince ourselves that we are incapable of learning and growing. I don't know about you, but that is quite a gloomy outlook to believe. Such an outlook will make it impossible for any individual to reclaim autonomy over their actions, which means they must allow their undesirable impulses to override their power. After that, an individual will have no choice but to depend on an external authority to restrain themselves. But because such a moral system is contingent upon the individual's conviction of being incapable of reform, such a system only works by continuing to diminish the individual's power. Thus, lacking true reformative value, extrinsic morality will eventually quash an individual's sovereignty over their mental faculties. Let me assure you, that is the last thing we want to do since evil actions are an offshoot of an individual's lack of control over their mental faculties. So, we will only add fuel to the fire or create a ticking time bomb when we create moral systems that diminish an individual's autonomy.

We should not assume that any code of conduct classified under morality is without any flaws that could impair an individual's ability to think or act freely, thus lead to an unhealthy dependency on a moral proxy or pure chaos. The protests in Iran after the death of Masha Amini while she was under the custody of the Morality Police illustrate that morals can be flawed. But even if we could have a perfect moral system, it will be of little use if an individual does not have the faculties to reason and therefore act freely within a moral system. With this in mind, we must not prescribe morality as the magic pill that will fix our shortcomings. Morals cannot fix every personal challenge that impairs or diminish our autonomy, but spiritual care and growth might.

In light of the recent pandemic, we now know what happens when we face an ailment that we do not understand. Our hospital beds quickly fill up. Those who oversee our physical care become overwhelmed as the unknown ailment ruins lives. Whenever the cause of any suffering is not clear, we cannot expect the answer to be clear. Thus, we may find ourselves on a spiral towards chaos and oblivion if we do not discover or understand the real cause. Figuratively speaking, this is the situation we find ourselves in with regards to our spiritual shortcomings.

We are fortunate to be in a place in time where due to mankind's scientific advances, we now have medical breakthroughs to help us combat our physical ailments. However, our spiritual shortcomings are more challenging to address since only the spirit can save itself. But how would you even begin to relay this concept to those who are oblivious of their spiritual nature? That is the trillion-dollar question!

Healing is restoring something to or close to its natural state of health. This means before we can attempt to heal ourselves spiritually, we must first understand our true nature. In other words, we can only understand the path towards healing when we understand our core individuality.

I have heard it said that "God has a *reason*" for whatever he does. I've struggled to understand this, especially considering the phenomenon of people who seem to be genuinely upset about being born in the wrong body. There must be an untold story that we are missing in this picture, wouldn't you agree? Anyway, I have narrowed things down to two possibilities from a spiritual perspective: either God is using these anomalies to break "the Matrix" if you will; or the spirit itself is sending out an SOS through these anomalies, like a castaway lost in the sea of time. I know this is just a theory, but can you say with absolute certainty that any of these two are out of the realm of possibility? I can't! At least not without assuming that there is no such thing as a spirit at all, and therefore no God. And not without concluding that past lives are not real, meaning there can be no residual memories from previous trinities to be misplaced in time, thus resulting in a mix-up of identities.

There is a common denominator between any spirit that is convinced that it's only human, and any spirit that believes it's born in the wrong body. They manifest different aspects of the same blind spot, and that is the inability to discern their true nature from *form*. Consequently, they cannot free themselves from the entanglement of form-driven identity and time. But whatever the case may be for each individual, we need to reestablish and affirm our core qualities towards which we can strive to become whole again.

I firmly believe that everything that ails us is indicative of an aspect of some core spiritual qualities that we have forgotten. Maybe God is like a mirror that is only supposed to guide us towards our essence, the purest Spirit in the hierarchy of spirits. Since, if God could command you and me to salvation, he could simply hit the "reset button," right? But we know that things don't work that way in life. Because without your willingness to redeem yourself, you will not gain any traction towards true redemption. Thus, only you have the power to save yourself ultimately by finding the core part of you that God reflects. This means that you must overcome feeling unworthy of God's likeness before you can embrace your divine nature.

Understanding that the truth is not something we can create with the magic wand of our beliefs is crucial to our discovery of the truth. We cannot force the truth to be what we believe. Since if we put our beliefs first, we will also unintentionally set ourselves up to distort the truth. Clearly, no truth seeker wants that! The truth simply exists, just as space exists. Still, since the truth is subtle and at the core of existence, we usually need to take apart the layers of existence in deep thought to find it. Sometimes the truth indirectly boils over as psychological anomalies or supernatural events. So, when such events occur, we must not rush to conclusions only driven by materialistic logic. Instead, we must learn to embrace what is, with the purpose of understanding. We must set aside our *desire* to be right. Because the desire to be right can turn into a self-serving mechanism that deflects the truth to preserve the toxic pride of ignorance. And such pride ends up being the bane of our spiritual redemption.

If you look at all that we have covered using the Spectrum of Conclusions Chart, I hope you can now see how a lie can have a palpable effect on your awareness. Likewise, the truth can also have a profound effect on your awareness. One will leave you feeling torpid, while the other will free and empower you with deeper insights about life. Thus, using the contrast between the impact of each of the two, we can have a pragmatic path towards spiritual truths that can nourish us, rather than let superstitious fears leave us feeling too paralyzed to live freely.

We are taught to fear God under the premise that we are only human. And guess what, the lie that we are only human puts us in conflict within ourselves. However, we may find ourselves being a bit more hopeful about the future than an atheist would be. Because our belief in God keeps us indirectly connected to our own true nature. If religion teaches us to fear exploring our spiritual nature as something evil or ungodly, we may end up shying away from asking the questions that reveal our essence. How would that lead anyone to spiritual salvation?

Without the spirit, form has no purpose. After all, it is the spirit that brings form to life, even according to the book of Genesis and according to the definition of a spirit. This is why I believe Jesus when he says we are gods in Psalms 82. Maybe not in the sense of creating everything, but in the sense of spiritual beings who have the potential to give life and purpose to form, while existing free of the limits of form and time. So, unless we take our rightful place in the trinity of our lives, existence will continue to be a mystery!

While loss is real, I believe death is only an illusion created through the abnegation of our true nature. The loss of form cannot end the existence of something that was there before the creation of any form. What powers the trinity of your life is you in your truest state. So, what's to say you cannot create another trinity once any form you possessed succumbs to time? The only reason you may think that this is not possible is the lack of affirmation regarding your spiritual nature. If you can overcome any beliefs, ideas, or perspectives that seek to blind you from your true nature, you will not need to worry about your future, because time does not apply to something that time itself depends on to exist.

The path towards our spiritual awakening is undoubtably riddled with superstition, irrational fears, lies, and false knowledge. It took me a long time to overcome my own religious fears and finally be able to connect the dots. Only then did I realize that even though religions package things differently, there were spiritual consistencies that I could not ignore. I found that me having any religious bias in such a case was just irrational. So, I decided to prioritize the truth.

In my early Christian days though, I used to fear asking questions in pursuit of the truth because I was led to believe that I was being disobedient to God, until I realized that even the "devil" does not fear using God's name to keep us gullible. As the saying goes, "misery loves company." So, the way I see it, making God seem unapproachable to us could very well be the devil's strategy to keep us in his own company.

I know that we each have our own spiritual paths to travel and obstacles to overcome. But fear of offending God while seeking the truth should not be one of those obstacles. Why would God be offended by your desire for truth? It can only be those who wish to keep you away from the truth who will be offended. Because the truth is the only powerful solvent that can set you free from the grip of their deceit. But without the truth, those misguided by form logic can convince you that you are only a complex composite of star dust, churned out by time!

In life, as we integrate our awareness with our body's perception channels, it becomes harder for us to realize that awareness is not necessarily an attribute of form. But let us assume for a moment that awareness was an attribute of form. What you will find is we couldn't even account for the origin of the faint awareness in dreams from that premise. So, to make up for the logic deficit, we must come up with the radical theory that dreams have something to do with our complex brain functions, whatever that is. But we know deep down inside that this theory does not compute. We may not have all the answers, but should that justify that we embrace any vague form driven theory that leads to nowhere except oblivion? I don't care how prestigious the halls of learning such fallacies may emerge from. They can keep their prestige all the way to oblivion. The truth must supersede prestige, otherwise we will blind ourselves from seeing the truth through our obsession with frivolous prestige.

The fact that we can imagine and manifest the things that we want in our lives, or shape reality with our ideas are only a few examples of how, even in our limited state, we can still influence form. If that is not a godlike potential, I don't know what is. Even prayer is nothing without our acknowledgement that the potential to manifest something out of "nothing" is real, no matter how spotty that potential might be in our current state! So, if you have had the good fortune of witnessing something you wished for manifest, seemingly out of impossible circumstances more than once, embrace that awareness! Embrace the faith and embrace the nature in which your wish came to manifest, then realize that it all started with you wishing for it! If you can see such events as miniature models of life on a bigger scale, then you may be able to see that what manifests in form emerges from a formless state, be it a goal, a wish, a dream, or an idea! So, we find ourselves facing a formless dimension that is capable of influencing form. That is the dimension of our immortality!

You may not always feel strong or powerful in this world, but never lose sight of what you are. I know that time may have caused you to doubt yourself, and loss might have made you forgetful of your true nature. So, I want to remind you that existence is part of your essence. You are not secondary to existence. You are the prime force that is vital to existence, even in your weakest state. Hold on to that awareness and rise up! There is work to be done for you to be whole again. And only you can find the humility to use what you know and trace your missteps to make things right. The ball is in your court now, I hope you make the most of it.

If you ever find yourself feeling anxious about your future, ask yourself how you are defining yourself instead, and you will find the answer. I know it's easy to feel out of place in this world. And I truly understand how lonely it feels to be misunderstood. But it is time for you to come forward and help put the world in order. Not everyone is ready to consider or accept their true nature. Regardless, we cannot elevate the world by neglecting our very own essence, or by being agreeable with those who have lost touch with their own. Unless you realize that there is nothing you can do to help someone unwilling to help themselves, your sense of compassion can darken with guilt. Feeling guilty for something that is not within your power to change will cripple you with despair.

It may feel cruel to watch those who believe that they are only human do so at their own peril. But if you have done all you can to help, you must acknowledge your limits to keep your sense of compassion pure. Only then can you keep your purpose alive and keep doing your part to elevate the quality of life. I believe elevating ourselves spiritually is the only way to elevate humanity. At this point, I hope you understand why I believe so. If you do, I will consider myself fortunate to have a kindred spirit with whom I can share the dream of a brighter future.

When all is said and done, I hope you will move on with your dignity intact and embrace your immortality in the glory of your restored essence. But for now, I hope that you will live your best life with all that you know and take on life powered by the anointing of truth. If we can find common ground in unforced truths, Earth could mirror heaven, like a warm smile mirrors our joy within. That, I believe, was once our shared dream!

CASCADING SPIRITUAL MAXIMS

Throughout history, mankind has made little attempt to codify spirituality beyond belief systems. This lack of rational codification of spiritual truths led to the rise of false beliefs. Consequently, being deficient in reason, facts, or truths, false beliefs empowered materialistic and evolutionary sciences. And now, we are at the point where evolutionary sciences can make a mockery of spirituality, thus disrupting the core of life. As of now, most major dictionaries define spirituality under the context of religion, which only limits the scope of spirituality to the choice of one's belief system. However, spirituality embodies the essence of existence and therefore deserves to be a field of knowledge in itself. It is for this reason that I propose the following definition for spirituality: *Spirituality is a branch of knowledge that deals with the fundamentals of existence, consciousness, awareness, knowledge, truths, and the influence of conscious activities over the material world.* An example of conscious activity is our ability to create technology. The purpose of spirituality is to search for, verify, and codify fundamental truths, characteristics, and faculties that are unique to the spirit (in contrast to form or matter), into a comprehensible body of knowledge.

A fundamental truth is a core factor that is indispensable from existence, thus true. Since we cannot separate consciousness from existence, yet it's not a function intrinsic to *form* or *matter*, consciousness is a great example of a spiritual truth. We must aim to establish and codify such truths into a system of knowledge that illuminate the nature and inherent faculties of the spirit.

According to the Merriam Webster dictionary, a maxim as a general truth or fundamental principle. Cascading maxims are therefore a set of general truths that flow or cascade from a central truth. I hereby propose the following cascading maxims to codify general truths that reflect the relationship of consciousness to existence:

- Life as we know it consists of physical and formless qualities.
- In all the physical and formless attributes of existence, consciousness is prime.
- Consciousness is essential to imagination, intelligence, knowledge, and creativity.
- Our ability to reason, know, solve, create, or purposely design, are faculties that rely on *conscious activity*.
- The ability to perceive objects is a faculty of consciousness. But what is perceivable doesn't necessarily constitute the truth or precede consciousness.
- Nothing is knowable outside the realm of conscious activity. Thus, existence to be knowable must be fundamentally *linked with* a conscious entity to make perception possible.

- A conscious entity must naturally possess the faculty for self-awareness. Sovereign existential awareness is thus the primary characteristic of individuality.
- Existence consists primarily of conscious activities. This includes thought, creation, perception, interactions, love, and other types of conscious activities.
- Since objects cannot engage in conscious activity, they lack the faculty necessary for self-awareness. Thus, conscious activity is what separates the spirit or life force from the physical or form-based aspects of life.
- Knowledge consists of detailed practical insights inherent to the conscious entity or acquired by the conscious entity through learning.
- Since we cannot formulate knowledge without the capacity for consciousness or intelligence, we can firmly establish that

fundamental to all that is knowable, there is a conscious entity.

- Individuality consists of our awareness of the extent of our existential sovereignty, our inherent potential, rights, ideals, and personal objectives.
- If the spirit neglects its role in existence, it diminishes its awareness, knowledge, or understanding of existence.
- Since the spirit cannot eliminate itself from existence, oblivion is the closest the spirit gets to fabricating its non-existence.
- The reawakening of the spirit starts with its enlightenment and the affirmation of its true nature and function value to life.

With these cascading maxims, we can start to map the characteristics unique to the spirit and have a better understanding of parts of ourselves that we've been trying to piece together and reclaim through our beliefs. Nevertheless, it's not enough for you to take my word for it. These maxims mean nothing if they do not represent life. So, I challenge you to disprove these maxims if you believe that consciousness is a byproduct of evolution. If you can prove that the energy that makes up form simply existed, then evolved into consciousness, uncaused by any conscious entity, I will consider spirituality a fallacy. But if you must disprove consciousness, you should do so without relying on any product or faculty of conscious activity. If you think that is impossible, that's exactly the point. Nothing meaningful emerges in the absence of conscious activity. These maxims may not be perfect, but if we can see the general truth in them, we can improve upon them as we learn more about our transcendent nature, so that we can be whole again. That is the goal of spirituality.

The ultimate spiritual trojan horse is a lie that seems to align with facts, while feeding off our spiritual ignorance to evade detection. You will find that you can't shake off such lies easily. The ideas that we are only human, or that we are just animals are perfect examples of such lies. When these lies are then ordained by science as the ultimate truth that should govern all our conduct, we end up with societies with individuals fated to obey their animal instincts only. Does this ring a bell?

The idea that consciousness is brain activity is a big lie! But since the proponents of this brain misconception have done a great job of selling their assumptions about the brain, we can be fooled by the sheer number of people who believe the brain has the power of consciousness. But that is not true. The brain is as conscious as a computer processor. That processor has to get its instructions from somewhere. So, the brain will either get its instructions from *you*, or from the environment through you.

One thing that I learned from coding is that before writing any code (computer instructions), you should know what task you want the code to accomplish beforehand. So, the idea that DNA is some kind of code that simply evolved without any conscious predetermination of its function is illogical! Unless we wish to ruin our capacity for reason, using evolution or the Big Bang theory to try and explain conscious activity only leads to irrational and self-deprecating conclusions.

It takes extraordinary intervention before an individual can escape that vicious camp of self-deprecating logic. This is why spirituality must be a body of knowledge consisting of fundamental truths, not just a belief system. Otherwise, we empower material sciences to continue to spread lies that keep the spirit fueling its own captivity. Any spiritual battle you will face is fundamentally against a lie. If you realize the truth in this, you will understand why you must put up a good fight for spiritual truths.

I want to thank you for investing your time in reading this book. I hope you found something that enriched your awareness and helped to restore a bit more of your spiritual certainty. Keep up the good fight for spiritual truths. We must prevail to realize all that is wholesome, including our spiritual freedom! The world needs a spiritual revival now more than ever. Let's normalize our spiritual nature as the basis of how we live, and not be subservient to our human alter egos. With that being said, I hope the truth empowers you to settle the battle against your spiritual nature once and for all! The truth is in your favor! But it's up to you to embrace it and claim your victory!

SPECTRUM OF CONCLUSIONS CHART

See chart description below.

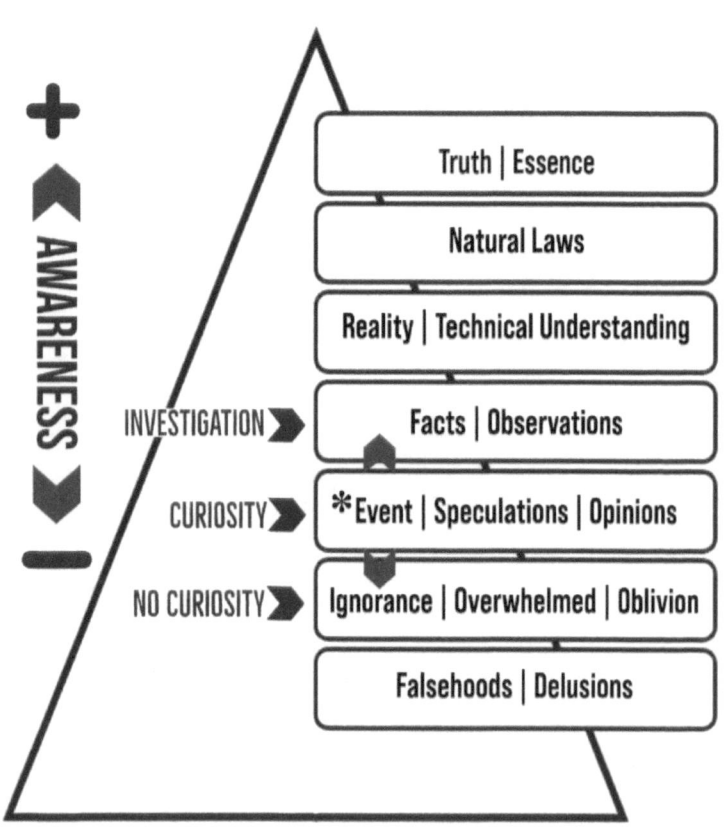

The chart above illustrates the spectrum of *conclusions* from various perspectives. It shows the relationship between other forms of conclusions and the truth. Any conclusion, if not the truth, limits our awareness. The general idea is that the higher we go, the more *clarity* we find. Truth is the highest possible conclusion we can achieve. *Curiosity* or lack of curiosity indicate *watershed* points for our interest in pursuing the truth after a fundamental question or a significant *event*. Therefore, our state of awareness is indicative of the choice we make regarding knowledge and the quality of information we consume and conclude upon about the nature of existence.

ABOUT THE AUTHOR

Tapiwa Chitembure grew up in Zimbabwe, immersed in the spiritual culture of the Shona people. His upbringing exposed him not only to Christianity and the cultural beliefs of the Bantu

people, but it also exposed him to pragmatic ways of thinking, in a culture that was evolving from superstitious beliefs to reason. After having an out-of-body experience at 10-years-old, he found himself with questions of which he could not find satisfying answers about his true nature. This void of answers is what set him on a path of curiosity to make sense of what felt like supernatural events. As he puts it, he went through an identity metamorphosis while trying to sort out truth from fiction.

Tapiwa writes about the insights that he gained in his search for answers, and how he found hope and perseverance through an understanding of his true nature. He shares that life has taught him that it takes humility to break through the blind spots that keep us from discovering life's truths. As a result, he believes that to find the truth, we must be willing to look at life from different perspectives. Only then can we see what remains, despite any of our apparent differences. To him, this humble approach is the most fruitful in pursuit of the existential truths akin to us.

ACKNOWLEDGEMENTS

I am grateful to America, a place that I now call home, its founding Fathers, and all those who have fought and are fighting to keep the spirit of freedom burning bright. You have created an environment where the truth can live and thrive. Without freedom of speech, the truth cannot thrive. I am deeply grateful that I can share my thoughts and observations freely, which helped to make this book possible.

I want to thank Kindle Direct Publishing, Adobe, and IngramSpark for providing awesome tools and resources that help authors like me manifest our creations. Your tools and resources made this book possible, and for that, I am thankful!

To my wife, Amanda, thank you for indulging my many passions. I appreciate your support and honest feedback. I love you and I am grateful for you! Thank you!

RELATED BOOKS BY AUTHOR

SUBTLE AFFIRMATIONS
The unorthodox beginnings of an amazing spiritual journey